Usborne Activities

How to draw
Fairies and
Mermaids

Fiona Watt

Designed and illustrated by

Jan McCafferty, Stella Baggott, Non Figg, Antonia Miller, Katie Lovell and Nancy Leschnikoff

Photographs by Howard Allman

Contents

Simple fairies

1. Use watery paint to paint a circle on a piece of paper for the fairy's face. Then, paint a simple shape beneath it for her dress.

2. Paint a wing on either side of the dress with watery paint. Paint the hair, then add a dot for the top of the wand. Leave the paint to dry.

3. Draw around the chin with a black felt-tip pen. Then, draw the dress and wings. You don't have to stick to the painted shapes exactly.

Paint lots of flowers and fairies together, like these, to make a big fairy picture.

Draw little lines around the star on the wand.

4. Draw her eyes, nose and mouth, then add lines in her hair. Draw her arms, making them overlap the wings. Then, draw a wand.

5. For a flower, paint large petals with watery paint. Add another blob of thicker paint on top, for the middle of the flower.

6. When the paint is dry, draw around the middle of the flower with a black felt-tip pen. Then, add petals around the edge.

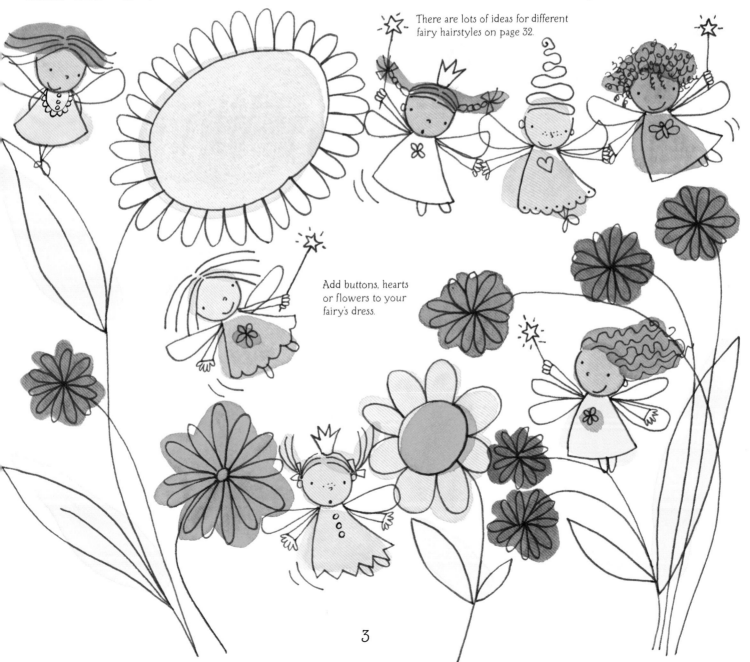

There are lots of ideas for different fairy hairstyles on page 32.

Add buttons, hearts or flowers to your fairy's dress.

Moonlight fairies

Paint lots of little dots for stars around the fairies.

Use chalk or a chalk pastel.

1. Cut a triangular-shaped skirt from white tissue paper, then rip it along its bottom edge. Glue the skirt onto a piece of dark blue paper.

2. Use white chalk to draw the top layer of the skirt on top of the tissue paper. Then, draw some white lines inside as the pleats in her skirt.

3. Cut another piece of tissue paper for the body and glue it on. Then, draw the fairy's wings in white chalk on either side of the body.

4. Rub the chalk to smudge the wings. This will make them look transparent. Then, draw around them again and add little lines inside, too.

5. Paint the fairy's neck and head, then paint two thin lines for arms. Then, paint lots of wavy lines for the fairy's hair.

4

For a glowing moon, draw a circle with chalk and smudge it with your finger. Then, paint the middle with yellow paint.

6. Draw a line with white chalk for the wand. Then, paint several little yellow lines coming out from the end of it, for a star.

7. When the paint is completely dry, draw her eyes, nose and lips with felt-tip pens. Add little pink ovals on her cheeks, too.

If you draw the fairies at different angles it will make them look as if they are flying.

5

Flying fairies

Paint a big pond,
then add lots of
fairies flying around.

You could draw some fairies
standing on lily pads.

Paint the hair overlapping the head a little.

Make the wings overlap.

Draw the stick of the wand on either side of her hand.

1. For a fairy flying sideways, start by painting her head, then paint her hair and dress. Add both wings above the dress, and a dot for the wand.

2. Draw around her face, adding a little nose and ear. Then, draw her dress and feet. Draw two leaf-shaped wings on her back.

3. Draw one arm on the dress and the other one below her face. Then, draw a stick for the wand. Add a star and wavy lines in her hair.

Looking around

You can make your fairy look up or down by drawing her eyes, nose and mouth in different places on her face.

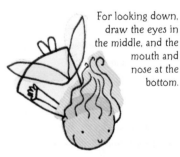

For looking down, draw the eyes in the middle, and the mouth and nose at the bottom.

To make a fairy look up, draw her eyes and nose near the top of her head. Draw the mouth in the middle.

Fairy flower garden

1. Cut out pages with lots of different pictures of pretty flowers from old magazines. Then, cut around individual flowers and some leaves.

2. Glue the flowers onto a piece of paper. Make some of the flowers overlap. Leave spaces between some of them, for the fairies.

Draw one or two fairies flying between flowers.

If you draw your fairy with her arms in the air it makes her look as if she is waving or jumping up.

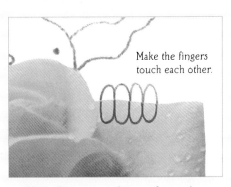

Make the fingers touch each other.

3. Draw the top part of a fairy's face peeking out over the top of a flower. Add the eyes and nose only. Then, draw the hair, too.

4. For fingers, draw four long ovals, touching each other. Make them overlap the edge of the flower to look as if they are curling over the petal.

5. You could also draw a fairy looking around the side of a flower. Just draw part of her body - the rest of it is hidden behind the flower.

Look on page 32 to see how to draw different expressions, like this surprised fairy.

You could draw around the wings with a blue felt-tip pen.

6. When you have drawn fairies between the flowers, fill them in with felt-tip pens or paints. Then, draw around them with a black pen.

Glue leaves under some flowers.

Fairy cakes

Use the ideas shown in this picture for decorating your fairies and cakes.

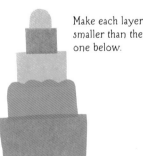

Make each layer smaller than the one below.

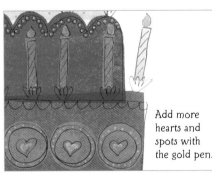

Add more hearts and spots with the gold pen.

1. Cut a rectangle of tissue paper for the bottom layer of a cake. Glue it onto some paper. Then, cut more layers and glue them on, too.

2. Use a thin black felt-tip pen to draw around each layer. Decorate each layer with different patterns, such as circles, hearts and wavy lines.

3. Draw holders for candles on some of the layers. Then, cut candles from tissue paper and glue them on. Add flames with a gold felt-tip pen.

10

You could draw fairies doing different things, such as lighting a candle or carrying a cherry.

You could decorate a cake with tissue paper cherries.

Draw a wavy line along the bottom of the dress.

Fill in the wand with the gold pen, too.

4. Cut a shape from tissue paper for a fairy's dress. Glue it near the cake. Cut two pairs of wings and glue them next to the dress.

5. Use a black pen to draw around the dress and the wings. Add her arms below the wings. Then, draw a neck and a curve for the chin.

6. Use a gold pen to draw the fairy's hair. Then, draw her face and add a wand. Decorate the dress, and her legs, with the gold pen.

11

Love-heart fairies

1. *Use a pencil to draw a fairy's head, adding two little ears. Draw her hair, then her eyes, nose and mouth. Draw the dress and add tiny feet.*

2. Draw a wing on either side of the dress. Make them look like hearts, lying on their sides. Then, draw arms and hands, on top of the wings.

3. Draw a wand, with the end part of it showing below her fingers. Add some hearts on her dress. Then, draw a heart on top of her head, too.

Add a band around her head.

4. Draw around your fairy with a black felt-tip pen. Then, erase the pencil lines. Fill her in with pens. Add a few hearts near her wand.

Draw the feet near the top of the dress.

5. For a fairy flying sideways, draw an oval head that includes a nose and an ear. Draw her eye, mouth and hair, then her dress and feet.

Draw a heart on her head, too.

6. Draw one arm on the dress and the other one out in front. Add a wand and a heart-shaped wing on her back. Fill her in with pens.

7. Draw a rough circle for a flower. Then, start to draw a spiral inside the circle. Make the lines go near the side of the circle, like this.

8. Continue drawing the spiral, making it overlap or nearly touch the other lines. Finish the spiral with a rough circle in the middle.

9. Paint the flower with pale pink paint. Then, fill in some parts with red. When the paint is dry, draw over all the lines with a black pen.

This background was painted in pale pink first. Then, the fairies and flowers were drawn on top when the paint had dried.

If you draw curved lines beside your fairy, they make it look as if she is moving.

Decorate your fairies with lots of hearts on their dresses and in their hair.

Draw lots of leaves around the flowers.

13

Rainy day fairies

Leave space on your paper to draw more fairies.

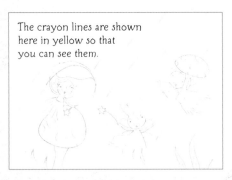

The crayon lines are shown here in yellow so that you can see them.

1. Use a pencil to draw a circle for the fairy's head. Then, add a dress with a wavy bottom edge. Draw her arms, legs and wings, too.

2. Draw her hair, eyes and eyelashes, her nose and a big smile. Then, draw little heart-shaped lips on the smile. Add a wand in her hand.

3. Draw more fairies in the same way. Add some leaves and toadstools, as umbrellas. Then, use a white wax crayon to draw lines for raindrops.

You could draw flowers and stars around your fairies and add some creatures, too.

The raindrops show through the paint.

4. Brush water over the paper. Then, brush watery pink paint on top so that it spreads in the water. Add some blobs of yellow paint, too.

5. When the paint is dry, draw over all your pencil lines with different felt-tip pens. Add patterns on the fairies' dresses, too.

6. Dip a thin paintbrush into water, then brush it over the pen lines so that the ink runs. Clean your brush after you do each part of the fairies.

You could draw a heart, instead of a star, on the end of a wand.

One fairy could be wearing a pair of glasses.

Dancing fairies

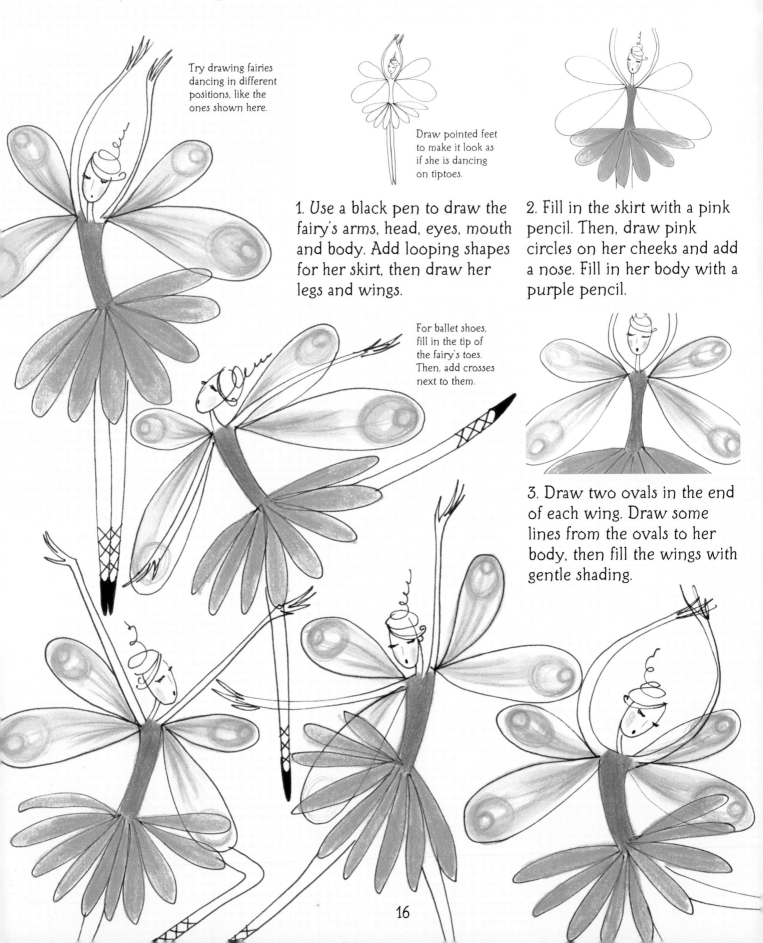

Try drawing fairies dancing in different positions, like the ones shown here.

Draw pointed feet to make it look as if she is dancing on tiptoes.

1. *Use a black pen to draw the fairy's arms, head, eyes, mouth and body. Add looping shapes for her skirt, then draw her legs and wings.*

For ballet shoes, fill in the tip of the fairy's toes. Then, add crosses next to them.

2. Fill in the skirt with a pink pencil. Then, draw pink circles on her cheeks and add a nose. Fill in her body with a purple pencil.

3. Draw two ovals in the end of each wing. Draw some lines from the ovals to her body, then fill the wings with gentle shading.

Fairy Queen

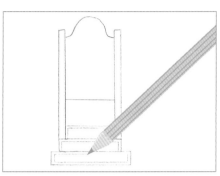

1. *Use a pencil to draw the* outline of a throne. Give it a curved top. Then, draw three steps below it. Add lines inside the steps.

Erase these lines.

2. Draw the Queen's head and hair. Then, add her dress and wings, overlapping the chair. Then, erase the pencil lines inside the wings and dress.

3. Draw the Queen's face and add a crown on top of her head. Draw her sleeves and hands on top of her wings, and add a wand in one hand.

Add some fairies around the throne. You can find out on page 5 how to draw fairies flying sideways.

Fill in your picture with paints or felt-tips pens.

Decorate the Queen and her throne with hearts.

You could draw flowers scattered around the throne.

Fairy paperchain

Make several fairy chains
and tape them together to
make long chains, like these.

1. Fold a long rectangle of thin paper in half, so that the shorter edges meet. Then, fold the paper in half again. Crease the folds well.

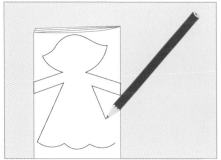

2. Draw a fairy's dress and arms on the folded paper, making sure that the arms touch each side of the paper. Draw a shape for the hair, too.

3. Cut around your drawing, but don't cut along the folds along her hands. Then, carefully unfold the paper to make a chain of four fairies.

These fairies were decorated with shapes cut from paper and a gold pen, too.

You could cut a star from foil instead of a fairy crown.

Cut out foil crowns and glue them on, too.

4. Fill in the fairies' hair and hands with felt-tip pens. Then, draw four faces on a separate piece of paper. Cut them out and glue them onto the fairies.

5. Draw stripes across the dresses with different pens. Then, cut strips of patterned paper from magazines and glue them onto the dresses.

6. Fold a piece of kitchen foil following step 1. Then, draw a set of wings against the fold. Cut them out, then glue them onto the backs of the fairies.

Mermaids on rocks

You don't need to draw around the painted edges exactly.

1. Paint the sea in watery blue paint across the bottom of a piece of paper. Then, paint two shapes for rocks above the sea. Let the paint dry.

2. Paint a shape for a mermaid's tail, overlapping one of the rocks. Paint a band for a bikini top, too. Then, add her tummy, face and hair.

3. Use a blue pen to draw around the tail and her top. Add her face with a black pen. Then, draw around the rock and add some lines for cracks.

Use the ideas shown here to draw mermaids doing different things.

20

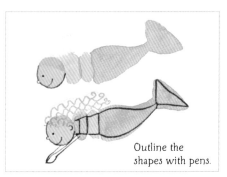

Outline the shapes with pens.

4. Draw one arm with the hand leaning on the rock and the other one waving. Draw little scales on her tail and add curly lines in her hair.

5. For a diving mermaid, paint shapes for the tail, body, hair and face, like this. Draw her arms reaching out in front of her. Outline all the shapes.

6. Paint simple shapes for the body and tail of a fish. Draw around them and add eyes, mouths and fins. Draw lots of curly waves with a blue pen.

Look on page 32 for lots of different hairstyles and expressions.

You could draw simple seagulls in the sky.

This background was painted with watery paints. The mermaids were cut out and glued on when the paint had dried.

The pearl that this mermaid is holding was drawn with wax crayon, then painted.

Diving mermaids

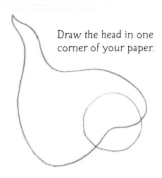

Draw the head in one corner of your paper.

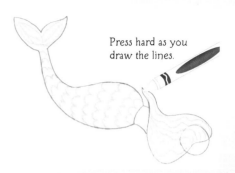

Press hard as you draw the lines.

1. Pressing lightly with a pencil, draw a circle for the mermaid's head. Then, draw a big wavy shape for her hair. Make it overlap the head.

2. Add two short curved lines for her body, coming from the back of the hair. Then, draw a curving mermaid tail.

3. Draw scales on her tail and wavy lines in her hair with a white wax crayon. They are shown here in yellow so that you can see them.

The crayon lines will show through the paint.

4. Paint the face and the mermaid's body. Then, paint two arms stretching out from her hair. Paint small shapes for her hands, too.

5. Mix some purple paint with water to make it watery. Then, paint the tail. Mix some orange paint with water too, then fill in the hair.

You could also paint shells and fish, and glue them onto your picture.

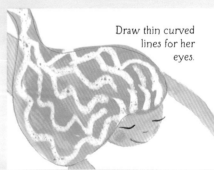

Draw thin curved lines for her eyes.

6. When the paint is dry, draw eyes halfway down the face. Add a nose. Then, draw her lips very close to the bottom of the face.

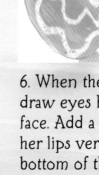

Mermaids' tea party

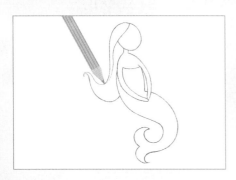

1. *Use a pencil to draw a circle for the mermaid's face. Draw her hair, neck and arms, too. Then, add a curling tail, as if she is sitting down.*

2. Draw her eyes, nose and mouth. Then, add a shell necklace around her neck. *Use an orange pencil to draw wavy lines in her hair.*

3. Draw a row of *U*-shapes across the top of the tail. Then, draw another row below, with the top of each *U* touching the bottom of the one above.

Use the ideas shown here to draw a mermaids' tea party, served by an octopus waiter.

4. Continue drawing rows of scales all the way down the tail. Then, use a pencil to draw a large shell for the mermaid to sit on.

The paints will bleed into each other.

Paint rosy cheeks, too.

5. Brush water over the paper. Then, paint blobs of watery green and blue paint around the mermaid and on her tail, but not on her face and hair.

6. When the paint is dry, mix some watery paint for the mermaid's hair and face. Fill them in roughly - you don't have to be too neat.

7. When the paint is dry, use pencils to fill in the mermaid's eyes, lips and necklace. Draw some patterns on the large shell, then add a swirl of paint.

8. Cut out two shapes for a napkin and glue them around the hands. Cut a picture of a cup or some food from a magazine and glue it on top.

The background was painted around the octopus, then it was painted and decorated.

Mermaids with silver tails

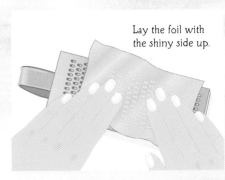

Lay the foil with the shiny side up.

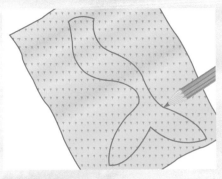

1. Cut a piece of kitchen foil and lay it on the medium size of holes on a cheese grater. Rub over the foil, so that the patterns on the grater appear.

2. Lift the foil off the grater and turn it over. Use a pencil to draw a curving mermaid's tail on the foil. Then, cut it out carefully.

3. Spread glue on the non-shiny side of the foil. Then, press it gently onto a piece of paper, trying not to squash the pattern on the foil.

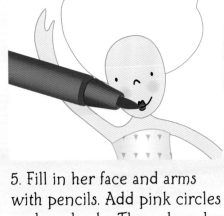

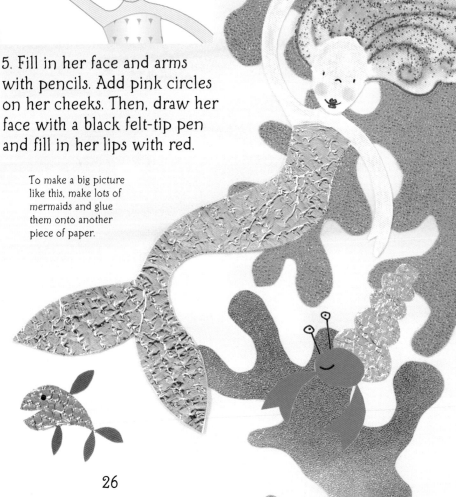

4. Draw the mermaid's head and arms above the foil tail. Then, draw a big shape for her hair, making it look as if she's floating in water.

5. Fill in her face and arms with pencils. Add pink circles on her cheeks. Then, draw her face with a black felt-tip pen and fill in her lips with red.

To make a big picture like this, make lots of mermaids and glue them onto another piece of paper.

The ink from the pen will spread.

6. Draw wavy lines on her hair with a felt-tip pen. Then, dip a clean paintbrush into water and paint it on top of the pen lines.

Cut wavy shapes for coral from shiny wrapping paper and glue them around the mermaids.

7. When the water has dried, spread glue over the hair and sprinkle it with a little glitter. Then, when the glue is dry, cut around your mermaid

Wave jumping

Leave some spaces between the lines.

1. Mix some watery blue paint. Then, scrunch up a kitchen paper towel and use it to paint wavy lines across a big piece of paper.

2. When the paint is dry, draw lots of curly waves with a blue pencil. Draw mermaids' heads above the waves and in the spaces.

Draw some curved lines on the ends of the tails.

3. Draw the hair, a neck and arms on each mermaid. Then, draw the body, stopping the lines where they meet a curly wave, like this.

4. Draw the end of a tail near each mermaid, poking out of the waves. Then, draw lots of wavy patterns, for scales, on the bodies and the tails.

5. Draw the mermaids' faces. Then, roughly fill in the mermaids' bodies and tails with purple, green and blue pencils. Fill in their hair, too.

6. Draw little fish in the gaps between the mermaids, then fill them in. Add some splashes of water around the fish and the mermaids, too.

7. Mix some white paint with a little water on an old plate or saucer. Dip a paintbrush into the paint, then hold it above the paper.

8. Flick your finger across the bristles of the brush so that the white paint splatters onto the paper. Splatter more paint again and again.

Mermaid door sign

The curly waves in this background were drawn with a white wax crayon, then paint was brushed on top.

Daisy

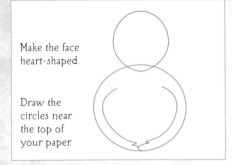

Make the face heart-shaped.

Draw the circles near the top of your paper.

1. Draw two circles. Make the bottom one bigger than the top one, and make them overlap. Draw a head inside the small circle and add ears.

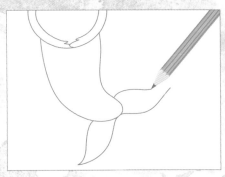

2. Draw the arms and hands inside the big circle. Then, draw a curved shape for the mermaid's tail and add leaf-shaped flippers at the end.

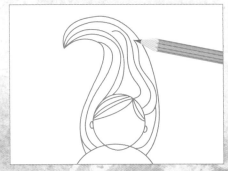

3. Draw the mermaid's hair, making it curl over at the top, so that it will hang on the handle of a door. Then, add some wavy lines on the hair.

4. Draw a shell between the hands, then add a curved line above it for the top of her tail. Fill her tail with rows of scales (see steps 3 and 4 on page 24).

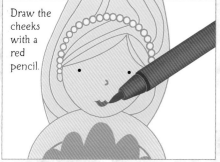

Draw the cheeks with a red pencil.

5. Draw a hair clip and a bracelet. Then, fill in all the shapes with paints or felt-tip pens. Draw her face with felt-tip pens and add red cheeks.

6. When the paint or pen is dry, draw around each part with a contrasting pen. Then, cut out the mermaid and write your name on her shell.

Nancy

Faces and hairstyles

This page will give you lots of ideas for drawing different expressions and hairstyles for your fairies and mermaids. There are also ideas for adding other details, such as earrings and hair clips.

Draw two lines for each eye, like the smiling face above.

Draw spirals for earrings that look like shells.

You can also draw spirals for hair tied in bunches.

The unhappy face below, has a shell as a hair clip.

For a surprised look, draw an oval mouth and fill it in.

You could add a headband around the hair and decorate it with hearts.

Try drawing long curved lines for sleek, straight hair.

Paint a blob for a flower hair clip, then draw a spiral on top.

Draw lots of wiggles for long wavy hair, like the hairstyle below.

For a crown, paint a blob of paint above the hair, then draw the crown on top.

Add a mouth that curves down for an unhappy face.

You could add rosy cheeks with paint or a pink pencil.

To make a fairy or mermaid laugh, draw an open mouth, like this.

For a princess fairy, draw a fancy crown and dangling earrings, like these.

You could draw a flower or lots of spirals in the hair for really fancy hairstyles, like these.

Draw curved eyebrows and an open mouth for another surprised expression.

For really curly long hair, draw lots of overlapping coils.

This happy face has two lines for each eye and a big grin.

You could draw a pair of glasses on some of your fairies.

Photographic manipulation by John Russell & Nick Wakeford • Flowers on pages 8-9 © Digital Vision
This edition first published in 2013 by Usborne Publishing Ltd., 83-85 Saffron Hill, London, EC1N 8RT, England www.usborne.com